DIESELS
— IN DEPTH —
Class 40

DIESELS
— IN DEPTH —
Class 40

DAVID CLARKE

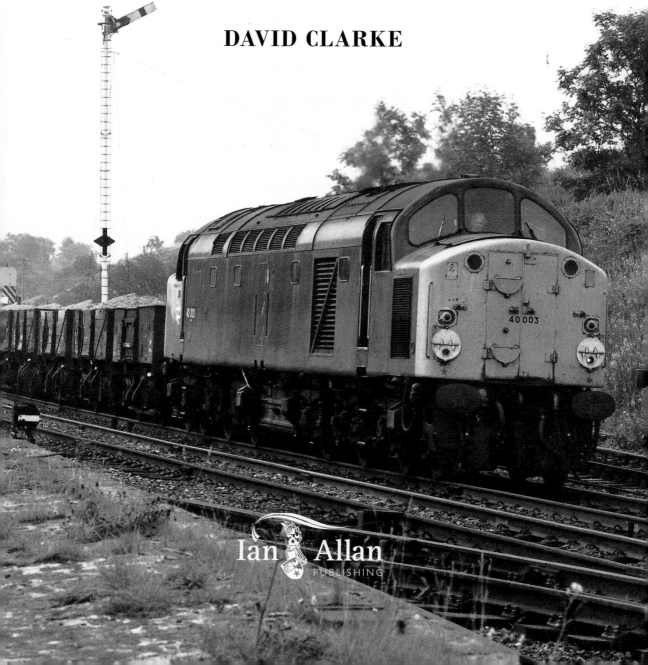

Ian Allan
PUBLISHING

Half title: No D202 passing Bethnal Green on 4 June 1958. *B. Morrison*

Title page: No 40003 heads north with a stone train on 4 August 1982. *R. Sharman*

Front cover: No 40036 waits in the engineers' siding at Skipton in the early 1980s. The photograph shows a number of modifications that were common by this period. *Author*

First published 2006

ISBN (10) 0 7110 3166 5
ISBN (13) 978 0 7110 3166 1

© Ian Allan Publishing Ltd 2006

Published by Ian Allan Publishing

an imprint of Ian Allan Publishing Ltd, Hersham, Surrey KT12 4RG. Printed in England by Ian Allan Printing Ltd, Hersham, Surrey KT12 4RG.

Code: 0606/B2

Visit the Ian Allan Publishing website at www.ianallanpublishing. com

Contents

Acknowledgements

This is the first in a new series of profiles of some of the 'classic' British Railways diesel locomotive classes, and in this case, one that has always been a particular favourite of mine and many other people. The reasons why Class 40 is considered so interesting are revealed, together with detailed information on why the type represents such a challenge to anyone wishing to make an accurate model.

My first contact with an English Electric Type 4 (subsequently known as Class 40) was in 1962 when I was aged 16, and I heard one idling at Wolverhampton High Level station as I alighted from a train at the Low Level station. I rushed up the steps to find out what was making this fantastic noise, and was faced with the huge bulk of No D235 *Apapa* standing there, its engine ticking over. Hearing it roar out of the station a few minutes later had me hooked on the sight and sound of the class. I still think, even in the first part of the 21st century, that they sound *awesome*.

An objective of the *Diesels in Depth* series is to illustrate the detail variations within each class covered, in an easily understandable form and where possible, using photographs annotated with arrows and descriptions. Tables are used to summarise the as-built configuration for easy reference, while subsequent changes are described in the accompanying text. One thing this is not, is another picture book full of three-quarter views of Class 40s in the landscape.

The photographs have been carefully chosen to show as many variations as possible within the class. The locomotive numbers used in the captions are the ones relevant to the period and style depicted. Where numbers are given for a particular variant, these are usually examples only as there may be other locomotives which also had this feature but have not necessarily been identified as such. Many variants may not have lasted for many months and were very often not recorded officially.

Wherever possible, I have used my own analysis for locomotive detail differences and these are the ones listed here. There are a number of lists in existence detailing which locomotives received which modification, but they may contain errors that have been perpetuated until they appear to become accepted fact, when this is not the case. Therefore, I have not used these sources and my evidence has been gathered by studying hundreds of photographs, with the maxim that if there is any doubt about a variant being carried by a locomotive, then it is not accepted.

A big 'thank you' is expressed to all the dedicated enthusiasts who have preserved a number of these magnificent machines and continue to put in many hours of effort to maintain them for posterity. I look forward to the day when my grandson William can hear the sound of a Class 40 for the first time and appreciate it. As he is only a year old at present he is a bit too young to understand the significance of such a noise!

I would also like to express my thanks to Dave Carter, a fellow fine scale modeller of some repute (of L&YR prototypes). He used to be a fitter at Wakefield shed in the last days of steam and subsequently at Healey Mills diesel depot, spending several years working on Class 40s, and has been able to fill me in on many details. I was able to find out what had changed on various members of the class at different times, but Dave could tell me *why* this had been done.

Also, thanks to Mervyn Allcock for allowing access to No 40013 *Andania* at Barrow Hill roundhouse and to Simon Stephens (a fellow Scalefour modeller) for help and for proof reading. Pete Waterman kindly allowed me access to one of his preserved nameplates (*Laconia,* made of resin) and shared the information on the story behind the 'nearly named' locomotive, *Media*. Finally, thanks to Glenis for all her support during the production of this book.

Bibliography

There have been a number of books published on the Class 40s, most now sadly out of print, but in the author's opinion, only one has ever really done the class justice, this being the John Vaughan title. However, this was published before the extinction of the class and there was a lot still to happen and to record subsequently.

The Last Years of the Class 40s. A. Wyn Hobson, Ian Allan Publishing 1985

Heritage Traction in Colour Volume 4. The Class 40s. Nostalgia Publications, 2005. A colour album of Class 40s, mainly showing members of the class in blue livery and near the end of their lives.

Profile of the Class 40s. John Whiteley and Gavin Morrison, OPC 1981

BR Class 40 Diesels. Malcolm Dyer, Bradford Barton 1982. A little booklet giving an overview of the class.

Class 40s at Work. John Vaughan, Ian Allan Publishing 1981. The most extensive book on the class with 128 pages (but no colour) and plenty of photographs. Recommended if you can find a second-hand copy.

The Heyday of the Class 40. Gavin Morrison. Ian Allan Publishing 2005. A colour album covering the life of the class.

The Power of the 40s. John Whiteley and Gavin Morrison, OPC 1978

In Memory of the 40s. Railphotoprints 1985. A softback compilation of Class 40 photographs, the majority showing locomotives in blue livery.

25 Years of the 40s. Railphotoprints 1983. A softback compilation of photographs by Steve Turner; an excellent variety of views even though the reproduction could have been better.

Book of the Forties. Norman Preedy, Peter Watts 1983. Depicts every member of the class in numerical order, again somewhat spoiled by poor reproduction.

INTRODUCTION

The bloodline for the English Electric Type 4s can be traced back to the late 1940s when both the London, Midland & Scottish Railway and the Southern Railway initiated projects to produce main line diesel-electric locomotives. The LMS work was based on its use of diesel-electric shunters built before World War 2. Following the end of the war, the new LMS Chief Mechanical Engineer, H. G. Ivatt, initiated collaboration between the LMS and the English Electric Company, to build two 1,600hp locomotives. The first, numbered 10000, appeared in December 1947, just three weeks before the LMS ceased to exist and British Railways was formed.

This locomotive was built at Derby Works with power equipment supplied by English Electric and whilst in many respects it looked very different from what was later to be the EE Type 4, it used one of the classic motive power units, the four-stroke 16SVT (16-cylinder supercharged V-form rail traction engine). This engine underwent a continuous process of improvement over the next 20 years and one of its descendants was used in the EE Type 4. Its use in Nos 10000 and 10001 (delivered in 1948) produced valuable information for the next generation of BR main line diesel locomotives.

The layout of the main components was similar to that used in the later Class 40, with the radiator assembly behind No 1 end, behind which was the diesel engine, and then the generator with the train heating boiler immediately before the No 2 end. The noses each contained a traction motor blower fan. The locomotive weighed in at 128 tons, some 5 tons less than the Class 40.

In parallel with the LMS developing No 10000, the Southern Railway was also working on a main line locomotive, which emerged as No 10201, on 30 December 1950, followed by No 10202 in September 1951. The Southern Railway's locomotives were produced independently of the LMS effort and displayed major differences in both body and bogie designs, much of which also influenced the EE Type 4. However, these locomotives shared with the LMS type the use of the 16SVT engine as their prime mover. Because of concerns about axle loading, there being no data available for that size of locomotive, the wheel arrangement was of a 1Co-Co1 design which gave three powered axles per bogie with an unpowered idler axle at the outer end. It is therefore ironic that the considerable length of the bogies of the Type 4 was to cause a number of problems with the civil engineer when they were introduced as they had no appropriate data for much of the pointwork on the system.

To compensate for the increase in weight, as compared with No 10000 (accounted for mainly by heavier bogies), the power output of the engine was uprated from 1,600hp to 1,750hp, made possible as a result of improvements to the turbo-charging arrangements. (The whistling noise of the four turbo-chargers led to the class receiving the nickname of 'Whistlers'). The turbo-charging on the Class 40 operated at a low pressure; only 4psi on full load compared with the 18psi of a Class 47, and this low pressure would not result in high power outputs from the engine. Following the introduction of Nos 10201 and 10202 there was a gap of three years before the third member of the class, No 10203, appeared in

April 1954. The opportunity was taken to incorporate many detail improvements including a small reduction in weight, it being 3 tons lighter than its two predecessors, and an increase in power to 2,000hp as well as small changes to the body — it did not have any nose doors for example.

The basic design of the Southern locomotives and the subsequent EE Type 4s always suffered a poor power-to-weight ratio which ultimately led to other designs having a better ratio, such as that of the Class 47 which took over express passenger duties, relegating the EE Type 4s to secondary passenger and freight duties.

Captured at York on 11 May 1981 was No 40192 with both the water tank between the bogies and the screen covering the radiator intake removed.
G. W. Sharpe

The 1955 Modernisation Plan proposed the replacement of all steam locomotives with diesel and electric traction and the initial order for 10 Pilot Scheme Type 4s was placed with English Electric, these appearing in March 1958. Numbered from D200 to D209, a repeat order was placed before this batch had been completed. The last member of the class was delivered in September 1962, making it four years to deliver a total of 200 locomotives.

Number	Builder	Date	Nose Type	Train Heat Boiler	Boiler vent grilles	Boiler Exhaust Port
D200-D209	English Electric Vulcan Foundry	March 1958	End doors, disc headcode	Stone	Long-Short-Long	Rectangular
D210-D239	English Electric Vulcan Foundry	1959	End doors, disc headcode	Stone	Long-Short-Long	Rectangular
D240-D249	English Electric Vulcan Foundry	1959	End doors, disc headcode	Stone	Long-Short-Long	Rectangular
D250-D259	English Electric Vulcan Foundry	1959-60	End doors, disc headcode	Stone	Long-Short-Long	Rectangular
D260-D304	English Electric Vulcan Foundry	1960	End doors, disc headcode	D260 to D266 Clayton D267 to D286 Stone D287 to D304 Clayton	Long-Long-Short Long-Short-Long Long-Long-Short	Circular Rectangular Circular
D305-D314	Robert Stephenson Hawthorn	1960	End doors, disc headcode	Stone	Long-Short-Long	Rectangular
D315-D324	Robert Stephenson Hawthorn	1961	End doors, disc headcode	Stone	Long-Short-Long	Rectangular
D325-D399	English Electric Vulcan Foundry	1960-2	D325-D344 split headcode boxes D345-D399 central headcode box	Clayton	Long-Long-Short	Circular

During the early days of the rush to build large numbers of diesels it was not unusual for work to be subcontracted and a small batch of Type 4s was constructed by Robert Stephenson & Hawthorns at Darlington to free up space at Vulcan Foundry to allow English Electric to build the 'Deltics' which were urgently required for the Eastern Region.

One of the first 10 Class 40s to be built is seen under construction at Vulcan Foundry, with its nose doors open. These were rarely used when in traffic and created draughts in the cab, much to the discomfort of the crew. *BR*

An unidentified Type 4 is seen under construction at English Electric's Vulcan Foundry, Newton-le-Willows. *BR*

No D208 on display at an exhibition at Finsbury Park on 13 September 1958, this being one of the first batch of English Electric Type 4s built. The bogie lubrication system can be seen under the driver's door as well as the plain-sided water tank between the bogies. Also of note, there are no handrails on the nose top. None of the first 10 was so fitted and this was always a distinguishing feature as these were never retrospectively fitted to Nos D200 to D209. *G. W. Sharpe*

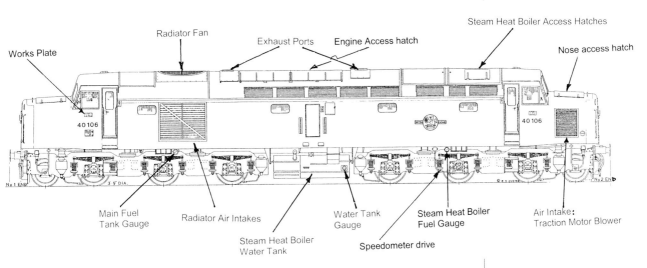

Works Plate

Radiator Fan

Exhaust Ports

Engine Access hatch

Steam Heat Boiler Access Hatches

Nose access hatch

40 106

40 106

No 1 END

3' 9" DIA.

No 2 END

Main Fuel
Tank Gauge

Radiator Air Intakes

Steam Heat Boiler
Water Tank

Water Tank
Gauge

Speedometer drive

Steam Heat Boiler
Fuel Gauge

Air Intake:
Traction Motor Blower

The objective here is to 'walk around' the locomotive and describe the various components and their functions. This is split into two sections: one for the body and the other for the underframe.

Bodywork and cabs

All diesel locomotives have a No 1 and a No 2 end. The No 1 end on British Railways diesel locomotives is always the radiator end and in the case of the Class 40 this is easily seen because of the large radiator grilles on each side of the body. The driver sits on the left-hand side of the locomotive, when looking forward.

When introduced, the locomotives had a two-man crew, the 'second-man' (who had previously been the fireman) being responsible for the train heat boiler. These arrangements reflected the fact that when diesels were introduced, many crews were working both steam and diesel locomotives for a number of years but no agreement had been reached at that time on single manning. This later changed, once steam had been eliminated from the network. The locomotive could be driven only when the driver had decided which end he required and had selected that end by a key-operated lock in the power controller and an AWS change-end switch on the cab bulkhead behind the driver which isolated the controls in the cab at the other end of the locomotive.

The nose at each end housed a large traction motor blower assembly which sent air over the three traction motors in the bogie to keep them cool. The location of the blower was shown by the grille on one side of each nose which allowed the fan to draw cold air from outside. On top of the nose were two hinged panels which gave easy access to these blower assemblies, allowing them to be lifted out when necessary. The nose interior could also be accessed from a door in the cab and through the external doors on the end of the nose, but both were a tight squeeze to pass through. The traction motor blowers created a vacuum in the nose end, resulting in the access door from the

The drawing by the late Russell Carter shows the position of some of the external features of the class.

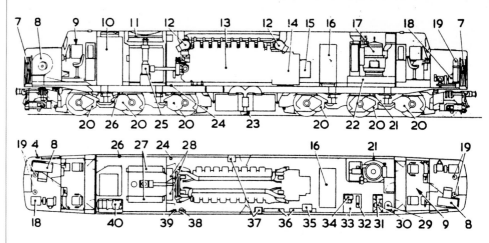

A diagram from the engineman's guide to the Class 40 illustrating the layout of the major components. *BR*

7	Flexible corridors	24	Cooling water filling connections
8	Electrically driven traction motor blowers	25	Radiator fan gearbox
9	Cabs (details given on Frame No. 11)	26	Fuel filling connections for engine
10	Engine fuel tanks	27	Radiators
11	Radiator Fan	28	Engine cooling water header tanks
12	Turbo-blowers	29	Toilet
13	Diesel engine	30	Voltage regulator
14	Main generator	31	Isolating switch panel
15	Auxiliary generator	32	Control cut-out switch
16	Control frame	33	Batteries
17	C.W.A. boiler (steam generator)	34	Main generator field regulator
18	Electrically driven exhausters for vacuum brake	35	Hotplate
19	CO_2 fire extinguishers	36	Resistances
20	Traction motors	37	Water tank filling ducts for C.W.A. boiler (steam generator)
21	Fuel filling connections for C.W.A. boiler (steam generator)	38	Fuel supply pump
22	Fuel tank for C.W.A. boiler (steam generator)	39	Lub. oil priming pump
23	Water scoop	40	Electrically driven compressor

A diagram detailing all the fitments in the cab. *BR*

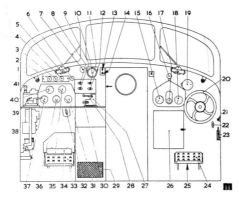

1	Window wiper control valve	11	Engine start switch	19	Pull handle cover (Fire fighting equipment)
2	Engine stopped indicator light	12	Engine stop switch	20	Hand brake
3	Wheel slip indicator light	13	Heater switch	21	Deadman's hold-over button
4	Fault indicator light	14	Nose compartment light switch	22	Horn valve
5	Window wiper motor	15	Steam pressure gauge	23	Vacuum release valve
6	Dimmer switch (instruments)	16	Water scoop control handle	24	Assistant's foot rest
7	A.T.C. reset switch	17	C.W.A. boiler (steam generator) indicator light	25	Heater
8	Sanding switch	18	C.W.A. boiler (steam generator) water tank gauge	26	Locker
9	Exhauster speed switch			27	Master controller
10	A.T.C. indicator			28	Main power handle
				29	Heater
				30	Reverser handle
				31	Air brake cylinder gauge
				32	Horn valve
				33	Driver's foot rest
				34	Deadman's pedal
				35	Main ammeter
				36	Vacuum brake gauge
				37	Main air reservoir gauge
				38	Straight air brake valve
				39	Air brake release trigger
				40	Speedometer
				41	Vacuum brake handle

The switches in the cab roof above the driver for controlling the various lights. *Author*

The two access hatches on the nose top. *Author*

The two access hatches in the nose top are seen here in the open position. These were used for removing the traction motor blower assembly for maintenance. *Author*

The nose end doors as built with all associated hinges and clips in place. The vertical handrails on the nose corners were not fitted from new but were added from the early 1960s onwards. The buffer beam is black, which was common when locomotives were repainted in blue. *Author*

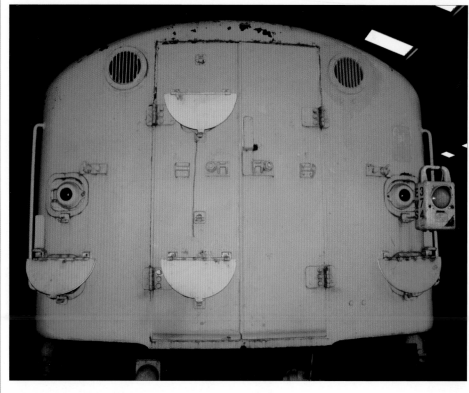

cab being sucked open and any warmth in the cab going straight down the traction motor blower duct. Drivers complained about the cold cabs and if they knew they were going to be working on a Class 40 would ensure they were well wrapped up. As will be described later, the doors on the nose ends were subsequently welded up and when air-brake equipment was fitted, some of this was located behind these doors.

At the side of the nose (No 2 end, second-man's side) there was a brass ring with a circular glass plate which housed the fire extinguisher operating handle that enabled the fire extinguishers to be activated from outside the locomotive by breaking the glass and pulling the handle.

The windscreen washer jets were protected from the attention of the fitting staff's hobnail boots by small steel brackets.

The locomotive's 700-gallon fuel tank was located immediately behind the cab at the No 1 end with very little external evidence of its position. Immediately behind the fuel tank was the engine cooling assembly, with the radiator on the second-man's side, located about two feet behind the external grille as there was a narrow, internal walkway down this side of the locomotive from one cab to the other.

Behind the protective honeycomb cover there was a slatted grille, the slats being movable, so that when the locomotive was parked in cold weather they could be closed to prevent cold air entering and causing damage, or for the engine to run too cool which would create problems of inadequate combustion leading to contamination of the lubricating oil. In practice, these slats were always left open. To assist in supplying an adequate amount of cooling air through the radiator, a large roof-mounted fan drew air through the radiator assemblies. This fan was driven mechanically by an extension to the crankshaft (with a gear ratio of 1 to 1) and therefore ran at the same speed as the engine, increasing in velocity as the engine accelerated; the increased engine speed would create more heat, therefore more air for cooling was required.

The external nose doors as seen from within the cab. The equipment blocking the access through the doors is related to the air brakes fitted after the locomotives were built. *Author*

Opposite:
The view looking down the internal walkway, through the engine compartment to the cab at the other end. The fuel tank is visible on the right with its prominent bolts for the inspection cover. The slats on the left are for the radiator air intake and the radiator on the right. *Author*

The front of the engine faced the No 1 end with the generator set at the other end. The steam-heat boiler, located between the generator and the No 2 end had its own tank of fuel oil. The electric control cubicle was located between the generators and the steam-heat boiler.

The V16 engine was fitted with four turbo-chargers and four exhaust ports (the engine was actually two V8s coupled together, but with a single crankcase), with the exhaust ports located at either end of the main engine cover.

Engine air-intake panels

A large diesel engine requires huge quantities of air — a 1,600hp engine such as this needs 4,000,000 cubic feet per hour — and this needs to be filtered to remove particles that would damage the engine through the air intake. On the Class 40, the air was filtered twice: once before entering the engine room and then before entering the turbo-charger inlets. The engine room was treated as a 'clean air' environment which meant that when the access doors into the cabs were closed, air could enter the engine compartment only through filters positioned behind the five slatted panels on the shoulders of the body. These panels were the same for all members of the class, unlike the three panels for the train heat boiler which varied in size, depending on the type of boiler fitted.

The slats on the radiator intake were movable by the crew and were designed to be shut when the engine was left running overnight in cold weather. The honeycomb outer grille has been removed, as evidenced by the bolt holes. Author

The doors located in the centre of the body in the open position. Above the two side handrails is evidence of the overhead warning flashes having been fitted on both sides. *Author*

Steam-heat boiler vents

The layout of these three vents, which allowed air for combustion into the area of the oil-fired boiler, was arranged as 'long-long-short' (Clayton boiler, fitted to Nos D260-D266, D287-D304 and D325-D399) or 'long-short-long' (Stone boiler, fitted to the remaining members of the class). These vents had filters behind them to reduce dust and debris getting into the boiler.'

This shows the air-intake slats for the steam-heat boiler, and the long-short-long configuration indicates the locomotive was fitted with a Stone-type boiler. If it had had a Clayton steam-heat boiler the slats would be long-long-short, so this is an easy way to identify which type of boiler was fitted. *Author*

No D354 on shed at March on 29 July 1963 with a small yellow warning panel as applied to locomotives with centre headcode boxes. The long-long-short boiler air intake vents (just behind the cab door) show it is fitted with a Clayton steam-heat boiler. A cast shed code plate is visible below the number at the far end. *G. W. Sharpe*

Steam-heat boiler exhaust ports

Stone boiler

This had rectangular exhaust ports and was placed immediately behind the cab on the driver's side. Two square hatches in the roof allowed access to the boiler and were hinged at the top.

Clayton boiler

Those fitted with this boiler had a circular exhaust port further back on the roof than the Stone type. The access hatches were rectangular and hinged on the side.

With the demise of steam heating, many locomotives had their boilers removed and the exhaust port plated over. To keep the weight balance the same, the train heat boiler was sometimes replaced with a block of concrete.

No D255 with the Stone steam-heat boiler being maintained and showing how the roof panels could be removed to aid the maintenance staff. The bogie lubrication system can be seen under the drivers door. *Ian Allan Library*

No 40086 heads an oil tank train at York in 1984 with the steam-heat boiler exhaust port providing evidence of use. As usual, the grille covering the radiator intakes has been removed. Class 47 No 47361 is alongside (complete with number on the nose). *G. W. Sharpe*

No D276 passes Mirfield with an express in June 1966. The locomotive is now fitted with a half yellow warning panel and two overhead warning flashes on the nose front. The exhaust port for the Stone steam-heat boiler is seen on the roof, behind the cab. Note the yellow axle box covers (without red stripe). *G. Morrison*

The circular Clayton steam-heat boiler exhaust port was located further along the roof than was the case with the rectangular Stone boiler-fitted locomotives. This is No 40035 on which the livery is unusual in that it has two BR double arrows on each side, as by this date (May 1976); the more usual style was only one per side. The top of the nose appears to be painted a light grey, or could it be faded yellow? *G. Morrison*

The access hatches for the steam-heat boilers varied depending on what type was fitted. This shows the hatches on a locomotive with a Stone-type boiler. *Author*

Cab interior colour scheme

This was dark green from the waist of the locomotive down, with the upper half and roof painted cream.

The bulkhead behind the driver and second-man. The door to the left leads to the engine compartment. *Author*

AWS timing cylinder. Gives the driver several seconds to acknowledge a warning before 'taking over' and making an emergency brake application

Fire alarm bell

AWS 'signal clear' bell

AWS isolating switch

Part of the AWS timing system

Drivers 'change end' switch. This must be in 'on' for a driver to use this cab

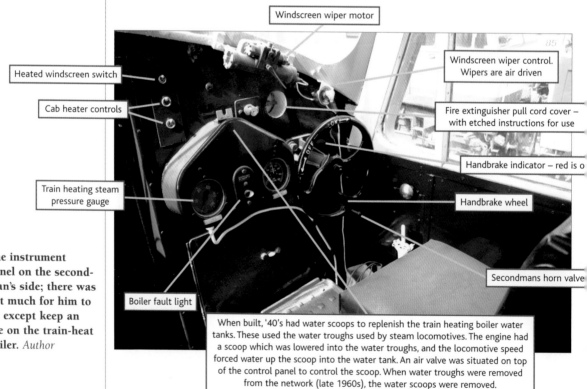

Windscreen wiper motor

Heated windscreen switch

Windscreen wiper control. Wipers are air driven

Cab heater controls

Fire extinguisher pull cord cover – with etched instructions for use

Handbrake indicator – red is o

Train heating steam pressure gauge

Handbrake wheel

The instrument panel on the second-man's side; there was not much for him to do except keep an eye on the train-heat boiler. *Author*

Secondmans horn valve

Boiler fault light

When built, '40's had water scoops to replenish the train heating boiler water tanks. These used the water troughs used by steam locomotives. The engine had a scoop which was lowered into the water troughs, and the locomotive speed forced water up the scoop into the water tank. An air valve was situated on top of the control panel to control the scoop. When water troughs were removed from the network (late 1960s), the water scoops were removed.

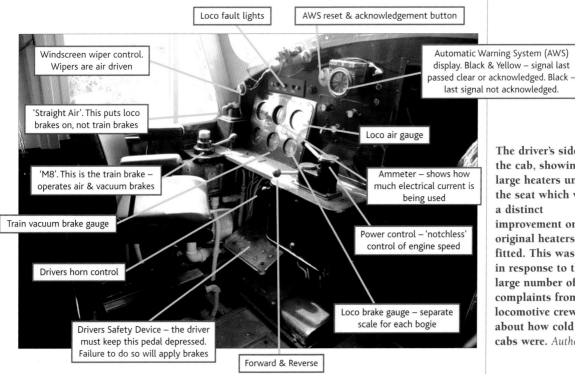

Loco fault lights

AWS reset & acknowledgement button

Windscreen wiper control. Wipers are air driven

Automatic Warning System (AWS) display. Black & Yellow – signal last passed clear or acknowledged. Black – last signal not acknowledged.

'Straight Air'. This puts loco brakes on, not train brakes

Loco air gauge

'M8'. This is the train brake – operates air & vacuum brakes

Ammeter – shows how much electrical current is being used

Train vacuum brake gauge

Power control – 'notchless' control of engine speed

Drivers horn control

Loco brake gauge – separate scale for each bogie

Drivers Safety Device – the driver must keep this pedal depressed. Failure to do so will apply brakes

Forward & Reverse

The driver's side of the cab, showing the large heaters under the seat which were a distinct improvement on the original heaters fitted. This was done in response to the large number of complaints from the locomotive crew about how cold the cabs were. *Author*

Underframe, bogies and running gear

The locomotive was built very much like pre-war cars, with a large heavy underframe taking all the loads and weight with a relatively lightweight body attached to it, this style of construction contributing to the heavy weight of the locomotive. The second generation of diesel locomotives which followed the Class 40 moved towards the same method of building as modern cars,

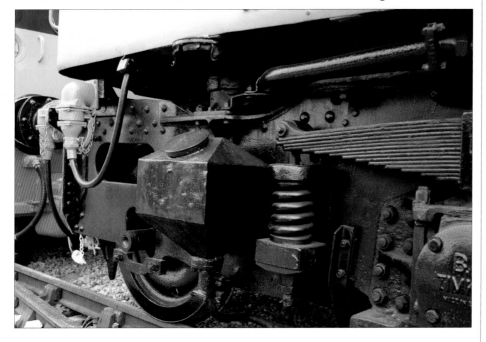

The body is supported on top of the bogie's by two curved sliding bearings (one at each end of each bogie) and the bearing at the front of one of the bogies is seen here above the sandbox. The axle end for the non-powered leading wheel set can also be seen as well as the body to bogie electrical connection. *Author*

No 40069
approaches York on
31 August 1977,
with its lower body
sides removed.
G. W. Sharpe

with a monocoque construction where the body is an integral part of the structure and shares the load bearing, resulting in considerable weight savings. The downside of this method of construction is that body corrosion can significantly impair the load-bearing ability. The Class 40 may have been heavy, but body corrosion would not affect it adversely. When the first members of the class arrived at Crewe Works for scrapping, the demolition crews referred to them as being built like battleships, and just as difficult to cut up.

Bogies

These were of massive proportions, being constructed of steel plate similar to that of a steam locomotive with the buffers and drawgear mounted on them. Each bogie contained three nose-suspended traction motors (the motor being attached to the axle as well as the bogie), and the motors, combined with the heavy plate frames, resulted in each bogie weighing 28 tons. However, the use of three powered axles and a leading non-powered axle kept the axle loadings comparatively low, giving them wide route availability. To aid the process of detaching the bogies when in works or at a depot, the multiple unit electrical connections from the locomotive to the bogie were joined into multiple pin connections on the side of the bogie, just behind the buffer beam. This arrangement prevented the type from snowplough working.

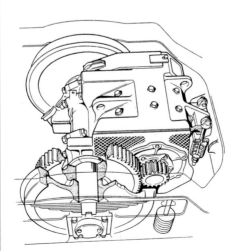

An official diagram showing how the traction motors are fitted within the bogie. *BR*

28

This is the corner of the buffer beam showing a small footstep bolted to the front. The air-brake pipes are white. The multiple working connection is an orange fitting to the left, between the bogie and the body. This was removed from a number of Scottish-based locomotives.
Author

This shows the fabricated step on the side of the bogie, below the cab door.
Author

No D324 displays a small yellow warning panel, two overhead warning flashes on the nose and yellow axle boxes at Crewe TMD (on the site of Crewe North steam shed).

G. W. Sharpe collection

The bogies were always horizontally parallel with the locomotive body and the only suspension movement was provided by the leaf springs on the side frames. This limited the vertical travel of the wheels and precluded them from running over humps in marshalling yards.

All the bogies were fitted with Timken roller bearings which, at various times, had the axle box covers painted yellow. This distinction was introduced when the BR Standard steam locomotives entered traffic to indicate to shed staff that these had this type of bearings rather than the usual plain bearings and would therefore require different maintenance procedure. Certainly, such painting of Class 40 axle boxes appears to have been very inconsistent with some seen in the mid-1960s, but most seem to have been black.

The bogies gave trouble throughout their lives with cracking being a major problem and when locomotives were nearing the end of their careers bogie cracks often led to withdrawal as repair by welding could be a long and difficult process. The problem was well documented with depots being issued with a diagram showing where the cracks were most likely to occur and specifying at what depth these would require works attention. The bogies were therefore examined regularly and if any cracking was found it would be steam cleaned and checked with a dye penetrant. If the cracks required attention the locomotive was normally sent to works and the fissure welded up.

The axle bearing oil boxes were filled with cotton waste coiled and packed in a specific manner, at a main works, and ran for many years without problems. However, a sudden spate of failures occurred and these had to be repacked at the depots. It transpired that the man at the works whose job this had been, had retired and his replacement was not fully proficient in the 'black art' of suspension-bearing packing!

The braking system on the bogie had two brake shoes on each driven wheel (the leading, non-powered axle was not braked), with each brake block having its own brake cylinder and adjuster to take up wear on the brake block. This self-adjusting system often did not work, with examinations finding that, say, only 15 of the 24 brakes were working effectively. It was not unknown for a Class 40 to run away when working heavy (and overloaded) engineers' trains. The handbrake was also ineffective as it was perfectly possible to drive off with this on and not be noticed.

The suspension movement for the Class 40s came only from the vertical movement in the individual axle box and spring assembly. There was no suspension movement provided by the bogie itself. The sandbox on the left (adjacent to the water tank) was removed from some locomotives late in their lives. *Author*

No D356 propels a brake tender at Healey Mills in the 1960s. Brake tenders were used for a short time to improve braking performance when working unfitted freight trains, but with the rapid decline of this type of stock the need for these vehicles also declined and they were later dispensed with. Although the Class 40s had 12 braked wheels, the brake performance was not good as the self-adjusting brakes usually required a blow from a hammer to complete the adjustment! *Author's collection*

The cab steps were complex fabrications as they had to fit around the coil springs. Here, the lids for the sandbox is missing. *Author*

Steam-heat boiler water tank

This was located below the middle of the locomotive and can be confused with the fuel tank by the uninitiated. It had a capacity of 800 gallons of water and was originally fitted with water scoops to allow filling on the move from water troughs. The scoop was located in the middle of the tank.

Capacity gauges

There were three sets of capacity gauges along the underframe, as follows:

a. Main fuel tank (oil), with the gauge fitted above the middle axle at No 1 end (under the main air intake for the radiators). Contrary to popular view, the fuel tank was not under the middle of the locomotive but inside the body, between the back of the cab (No 1 end) and the radiator assembly.

b. Water tank. This was hung underneath the middle of the locomotive and supplied water to the steam-heat boiler and was fitted with its own gauge.

c. Steam-heat boiler fuel tank. The gauge for this tank was just above the middle axle of the bogie under the No 2 end. The tank was inside the body and had a capacity of 200 gallons.

As part of the routine when a driver signed on and readied the locomotive for service, he would walk down both sides of it and check the status of these gauges.

The water tank for the steam-heat boiler showing the horizontal strengthening ribs and capacity gauges. The first 100 locomotives were originally built with plain-sided tanks, the ribbing being added later. Note the footstep welded to the middle of the tank. Many locomotives had an additional step provided when their water tanks were removed. *Author*

An axle box below the radiator air intake, with the main fuel tank gauge also in view. *Author*

Speedometer drives

The locomotives were fitted with the same Smith Stone speedometer drive as seen fitted on a number of steam locomotive classes. This was an electric generator mounted on the axle box, driven by the axle and producing a dc voltage with a voltmeter in the cab calibrated in miles per hour.

From the generator a flexible conduit ran up to a compensation unit, as from new to scrapping size, wheels could vary from 3ft 9in down to 3ft 6in, following wheel turning. After wheel turning the generator would be run by a calibrated drive motor and the compensation (resistor) unit adjusted to give the correct indicated speed on the driver's desks.

A detail view of the Smith Stone speedometer and the fuel gauge for the steam-heat boiler. *Author*

Distance recorder

On the middle axle of the No 1 end bogie on the second-man's side of the locomotive, there was a mileage recorder which had a hinged cover, underneath which was the mileage reading. Some components were overhauled on usage (the engine being measured in 'engine hours' run), but other items were measured by miles run (just as with a car).

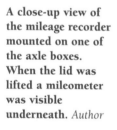

A close-up view of the mileage recorder mounted on one of the axle boxes. When the lid was lifted a mileometer was visible underneath. *Author*

Bogie lubrication system

When originally built the class was fitted with a mechanical lubrication system utilising a drive shaft from the axle box under the driver's door, to a mechanical lubricator by the bogie step. The shaft was protected by a cover bolted to the step. The whole assembly and the cover plate on the step were removed during the late 1960s, although some could still be seen in place as late as 1967. The reason for removal was due to oil residues and brake dust building up which could result in a bogie fire occurring. When the unit was removed, some of the lubrication was changed to grease which required certain parts to only be lubricated when the locomotive was in a works. In this way, responsibility for bogie lubrication passed to depot fitters and works maintenance staff and away from the driver. This proved successful and the number of bogie fires decreased.

When originally built the locomotives had a mechanically driven bogie lubrication system with a drive shaft to the lubricator mounted on the steps below the cab door and behind a cover plate. This system was later removed. A detail view of No D314. P. H. Groom

Air-brake fitment

During the late 1960s and early 1970s, air brakes were fitted to most Class 40s, but not all, with the associated additional pipes mounted on the buffer beam. The locomotives then became dual fitted as they retained their vacuum brake system. As this also necessitated internal pipework changes the first locomotive fitted, No D269, had part of the lower body side removed to allow access to the oil drainage pipes. Fortunately, this drastic body surgery was not repeated on subsequent locomotives fitted with air brakes. The installation of the air-brake equipment added another ton to the weight of the locomotive, taking it to 134 tons.

The front buffer
beam as fitted with
air-brake equipment.
Author

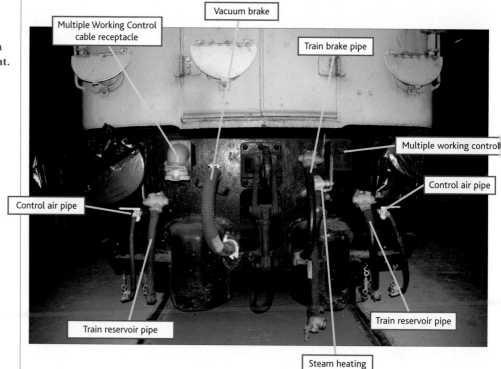

Vacuum brake

Multiple Working Control
cable receptacle

Train brake pipe

Multiple working control

Control air pipe

Control air pipe

Train reservoir pipe

Train reservoir pipe

Steam heating

Boiler water tanks

The first 100 or so locomotives were delivered with water tanks which had smooth sides. The remainder had two horizontal ribs on the side of the tanks, presumably for strengthening as the tanks would be under considerable pressure when picking up water from water troughs. For the first 100 locomotives the smooth-sided

The steam-heat boiler safety valve blows off as No D300 waits at Leeds City on 24 March 1962. The water tank is the original plain-sided variety, the tanks later being reinforced with horizontal ribs. The mechanical bogie lubrication system is seen below the nearside cab door.
G. W. Sharpe

As originally built, the water tank for the train-heat boiler for the first 100 locomotives had plain sides. This was subsequently modified with horizontal ribbing added to the outside, presumably to reinforce the tanks for when picking up water using the water scoop. A detail view of No D265. *HMRS*

The modified water tank with horizontal ribbing was fitted from new for the second 100 locomotives. A detail view of No 40077. *S. V. Blencoe collection*

tanks were either replaced or modified by the mid-1960s, although some examples were still fitted with plain tanks in 1963; No D216 for example.

From September 1968, following the demise of steam traction, the water scoops were isolated and then removed as there were no longer any water troughs in operation.

Boiler water tanks – removal

From 1979, a number of locomotives had the steam-heat boiler water tanks removed, leaving an unsightly gap underneath the locomotive. This was done as the need for steam heating was reduced and reflected the move of the class into freight working. With the removal of the tank an additional step had to be fitted to allow access to the centre door. A total of 34 locomotives were reported as having been converted, and from photographs, the following are known to have received this modification: Nos 40001, 40008, 40009, 40010, 40015, 40020, 40022, 40036, 40037, 40073, 40079, 40099, 40131, 40135, 40137, 40145, 40152, 40177, 40180, 40183, 40192, 40194, 40195 and 40196.

Sometimes, when the water tanks were removed a small 'NB' was painted below the data panel or under the locomotive number, to warn the driver that there was 'No Boiler', in case the locomotive was diagrammed for a passenger train that would require train heating.

No 40195 at Gateshead with its water tank removed. The shed code is below the data panel, both under the running number.
G. W. Sharpe

The now-preserved No 40135 stabled at Garston, Liverpool, in BR days showing the water tank between the bogies removed and the additional step fitted to replace the step on the water tank. Overhead warning flashes have now been fitted to the side of the cab doors, the grille covering the radiator intake has been removed and only rust patches show where the builder's plates were fitted under the cab windows.
Author's collection

No 395 at Wigan when still in green livery but with full yellow ends and what appears to be a yellow top to the nose. A shed plate is fitted below the number and between the two is 'NB' to indicate 'No Boiler' (steam heat) is fitted. The 'D' prefix to the number has been removed.
Author's collection

Passengers
must not cross
the line

Headcode disc removal

A number of locomotives were observed in the 1980s running with the discs removed, but the lights left in place. Examples included Nos 40001, 40003, 40009, 40010, 40012 (1983), 40013 (1980), 40033, 40035, 40058, 40073 (1980), 40084, 40085 (June 1981), 40087 (1982) and 40092.

Frost grilles

As built, the slatted air intakes were covered by an outer grille, usually referred to as a frost grille. This consisted of $^3/_{16}$in steel plate which had hexagonal holes punched through it. In service, these holes could become clogged with dirt which impeded the flow of air through to the radiators. At some depots these grilles were steam cleaned to get rid of the build up of dirt, but during the 1970s the Eastern Region took the view that the honeycomb grilles should be removed to improve airflow. Therefore, many locomotives then allocated to that region could be seen without the frost grilles. Whilst the Scottish Region followed suit, the London Midland Region was not convinced, and left the grilles in place. With transfers from the Scottish and Eastern regions to the LMR a number of locomotives with the grilles removed had them reinstalled. However, ultimately most of the class ran without them, although No 40106 retained them and No 40122 (D200) had the grilles refitted during its restoration at Toton depot.

The honeycomb grille which covered the radiator intakes. These were sometimes referred to incorrectly as 'frost grilles'. *Author*

Nose front ladders

These were fitted from No D210 onwards to provide access to the hinged hatches on top of each nose. The hatches were primarily used to allow for the removal of the traction blower motors. For other maintenance jobs within the nose, access was provided from the door inside the cab. These ladders did not last long, however, and most were removed by early 1962, presumably as a safety measure in view of the increased running under overhead wires. However, as with all things Class 40, some variants survived much longer and No 253 was observed in 1970 still with a nose ladder, complete with full yellow nose and the 'D' prefix of its number painted out. Locomotives observed with nose ladders included Nos D210, D211, D219, D223, D236 (1960), D244 (1962, with small yellow warning panel), D249, D251, D252, D261, D266 (1961), D268 (1961), D274 (1961), D279 (1961) and D308. The author has not been able to determine how many locomotives were actually fitted with nose ladders.

No D261 at Edinburgh Haymarket shed showing the nose ladder fitted to No D210 onwards. These were subsequently removed on most of the class by 1962 although one was still fitted to No 253 as late as 1970.
R. K. Blencowe

No 253 is seen at March in April 1970 still fitted with a nose ladder which had been removed from most of the class by 1962. The locomotive is in green with full yellow ends and has a data panel under the number at the far end. *Colour-Rail CTLS240*

Handrails on nose fronts

When built, the disc headcode and split headcode box locomotives were not equipped with handrails on the nose ends. The centre headcode examples (Nos D345 to D399) were built with short handrails on either side and above the indicator box. Following removal of the nose ladders, handrails began to appear on the nose ends, one at each corner, as follows.

No D279 at Leeds City on 2 June 1966 with the top of the small yellow warning panel level with the top of the marker lights (some panels finished lower down), and the two overhead warning flashes. The locomotive has acquired handrails on the corners of the nose and has black-edged headcode discs. The Gateshead shed plate (52A) has been mounted under the running number. *G.Morrison*

No 40042 in June 1978 with an additional vertical handrail to the right of the nose door, which was fitted to a small number of Class 40s. *G.Morrison*

No D226 at Grayrigg on the West Coast main line on 3 October 1959, displaying features as built, including a nose ladder and plain sides to the water tank. The nose top has two small hand holds.

G. W. Sharpe

Headcode disc

The first date I have photographic evidence of handrails being carried is June 1962 when No D242 was observed with a single vertical handrail on the nose front, just off-centre (driver's side). Subsequently, this locomotive was noted with handrails on the nose corners and No D243 was seen in August 1962 with similar fittings. The two handrails were located at the corners of the nose on both sides. The fitting of these handrails seems to have been quite a protracted process as many were still not fitted in 1964/65. A small number of engines were observed with an additional vertical handrail in the same position as seen on No D242. Examples included Nos 40041, 40042 and 40086.

Split headcode boxes

These do not appear to have been fitted with handrails at all, other than for two small handrails on the top of the indicator boxes.

With split headcode, No D338 is in green livery with a small yellow warning panel and a blue bar below the running number indicating it has had a change of traction motors.
Colour-Rail CTSL248

Centre headcode

These were delivered with short handrails at each side of and above the indicator box. In line with the headcode disc examples they acquired long handrails at the corners of the nose ends. This process seems to have been quite slow as No D369 was still not so fitted in 1966.

No D261, photographed at Edinburgh in July 1965, has been modified with the addition of the centre headcode box (having been built with disc headcodes). These modified headcode boxes could be identified by the square corners. The style of small yellow warning panel was unique to the Scottish-based locomotives with the modified centre headcode box. The locomotive retains its multiple working connections, which were removed from most of the Haymarket-based locomotives.
G. W. Sharpe

Handrails on the nose top

With the exception of the first 10 locomotives built, all the disc headcode locomotives were fitted with a pair of small handrails immediately in front of the two access panels on the top of the nose. These were also fitted to centre headcode examples, but not to the split headcode locomotives.

No D242 was photographed on 20 June 1962 when it was one of the first applications of a vertical handrail to the nose, in this case one to the right of the nose door. Subsequently, additional vertical handrails were fixed to the corners of the nose and only a small number of Class 40s carried this additional vertical handrail.
G.Morrison

No D206 at York on 3 August 1963 displays some of the modifications applied to the class: small yellow warning panel, ribbing to the water tank, and single overhead warning flashes to the nose front. As part of the first batch of 10 it does not have the two small hand holds on the nose top. The bogie lubrication system is still fitted.
G. W. Sharpe

Headcode boxes

A small batch of headcode disc-fitted locomotives allocated to Edinburgh Haymarket shed (Nos D260 to D266) were fitted with central headcode boxes, replacing the gangway doors in the process. These were subtly different to those built from new with centre headcode boxes, as they had square corners, rather than the more usual rounded corners. These locomotives were also distinguished by a

No D260 at Millerhill Yard in July 1970 in green livery with full yellow warning panel and a data panel below the running number. It was one of the members of the class allocated to Edinburgh Haymarket which were originally built with disc headcodes and converted to centre headcode boxes and the multiple working connections removed. The bogie lubrication system is still fitted and there are no overhead warning flashes.
Colour-Rail CTSL239

lack of handrails. Later in their lives, three of these locomotives (renumbered 40060, 40061 and 40065) received modified headcode boxes with rounded corners.

The origins of the end doors were evident after they had been welded up (and all the stops and clips removed) by the small lip at the bottom of the bodywork.

No D297 in green livery has a data panel under the number. There is no blue star on the nose front but there are two overhead warning flashes. On the right is an unidentified split-headcode locomotive with four overhead warning flashes on the front.

Removal of multiple-control jumpers

This equipment was initially removed by the Scottish Region and the following were subsequently observed: Nos 262, 40060, 40061, 40062, 40063, 40064, 40065, 40066, 40148, 40157, 40158, 40159, 40160 and 40161. Both the buffer beam connections and that between the bogies and body were removed. Also, the bottom of the nose just above the buffer beam no longer displayed the blue star which signified multiple working connections, as this was not applicable.

One of Edinburgh Haymarket's long-term residents, No 40160 on 5 September 1980, with the multiple working cables removed from the front of the bogie side frame and the buffer beam. This was done to most, if not all, the Haymarket allocation.
G.Morrison

Electric train heating (ETH)

For a short time, No D255 was fitted with electric train heating with its associated fittings on the buffer beam and the multiple jumper connections were removed. Once the tests had been completed the ETH equipment was removed and the multiple-control cables (and blue star) were reinstated.

Welding up of nose end doors

With the nose doors no longer required, many depots welded them up to eliminate the considerable draughts experienced by the crews, but there was little consistency in how this was done, and in many cases only one end was dealt with. Locomotives known to have been modified in this way include No 40067, 40098 (both ends) and 40027 at one end only.

Some of the variants were as follows: Nos 40002 and 40111 had all the doors, hinges and retaining clips removed and a plate welded in place and the welds ground down such that there was no evidence that doors had ever been fitted.

Nos 298 and D316 had the doors and hinges removed and a plate welded in place and ground back making a neat job, but the retaining clips were retained. No 40058, in contrast, was a rough job in the extreme with a large rectangular plate bolted over the space where the doors had been and the bolt heads holding the plate were very prominent.

Blanking plate over the boiler exhaust ports

With the requirement to provide steam heating eliminated and many locomotives having the boiler water tank removed, a number had the exhaust port for the steam-heating boiler covered over with a blanking plate. Examples included Nos 40036, 40037, 40073, 40092, 40127, 40141, 40170 (1983) and 40192 (1983). Unfortunately, most photographs do not show enough of the roof to determine if this modification had been made.

A detail view of No D246 at Cleethorpes in 1967 showing a blanking plate over the boiler port. *G. W. Sharpe*

Removal of sandboxes

Some locomotives had the inner set of four sandboxes removed from the bogies (those closest to the water tank). Examples included Nos 40006, 40028, 40038, 40044, 40046, 40055, 40060, 40091, 40103 and 40112.

No 40044 at rest at **Manchester Longsight** depot in November 1983, its sandboxes adjacent to the water tank having been removed as has the grille covering the radiator intake. It has a red surround to the fire extinguisher operating handle on the nose side. *G. W. Sharpe*

No 40091 on 25 April 1976 with the sandboxes either side of the water tank removed. Additional overhead warning flashes have been fitted adjacent to the cab doors. The grille cover to the radiators is still fitted and the body side shows signs of oil staining.
G. W. Sharpe

Repair of crash damage

This would sometimes create differences between one end of the locomotive and the other, such as on Nos D327 (40127) and 40131 built with split headcode boxes but fitted with a nose with end doors and disc-type indicators at No 2 end during the 1970s (probably as a result of accident damage). In the case of No 40131 there was a further variant in that the disc-type indicators were later removed along with the lights leaving two pockets in the end door.

When train reporting numbers ceased to be displayed, most members of the class were fitted with 'domino' panels showing two circular lights. However, Nos 40062 and 40158 both received plated-over headcode panels with marker lights at their No 2 end.

No 40131 departs from Llandudno Junction in 1982, with a nose door that was previously fitted to a disc headcode locomotive now on its left-hand side. With the lights removed it gives the appearance of two hand holds in the door. *G.Morrison*

No 345 with damaged nose, awaiting repair at York depot in April 1970. *G. W. Sharpe*

Windscreen washer jet covers

This was one of the less obvious changes as it is difficult to spot in photographs. It soon became apparent that fitters climbing on the nose tops and then onto the cab roof were damaging the small (and comparatively fragile) windscreen washer jets with their hobnail boots. To minimise this damage a simple, steel cage of 1in strip was made to fit over the jet to protect it. It is not known when these were fitted or if they were added to all Class 40s.

Removal of cab roof ventilators

The small circular ventilator on the cab roof appears to have been removed from Nos 40163, 40164, 40166, 40167, 40168 and 40180 which was also observed without the cab ventilator in 1965. As all these locomotives were based on the Scottish Region it can only be assumed that this was a local variant, but why and where the work was done is not known to the author. The class had a well-earned reputation when first introduced of being very draughty and cold, and subsequently more effective cab heaters were fitted, so it may be this modification was made to reduce some of the draughts. Certainly, locomotives from the same batch on the same shed (Haymarket, Edinburgh) such as No D261 were originally fitted with ventilators as this engine was seen with one in 1965.

Hatch for air-brake equipment

Three locomotives had one of the body side windows replaced with a side-hinged hatch to allow access to the air-brake equipment, when fitted in 1965. The locomotives fitted were D370 (40170), D371 (40171) and D380 (40180).

No 290 is seen at Crewe revealing how badly the green livery was allowed to deteriorate before repainting into blue took place. The data panel is seen below the number at the far end and the builder's plates appear to have been removed.
Locophoto Co

BR green

When delivered the locomotives were painted in the same Brunswick green as used on express passenger steam locomotives, but without the orange and black lining (although this had been applied to No 10203). The body side at the top, just below the roof (the cant rail) had a light blue/grey stripe along the length of the locomotive. The standard post-1957 British Railways emblem (universally known as the 'Ferret and Dartboard') was applied one on each side towards the No 2 end. When the locomotive was named, the nameplate was located between the centre door and the radiator grille at No 1 end. The roof was painted grey and the buffer beams red.

Three locomotives in the class never received blue livery: the hapless No D322 destroyed in a crash in 1966, No 40039 (one of the early withdrawals) and No 40106 which retained its green livery after a works visit, for use on enthusiast trains and excursions. No 40106 was still in green, but very faded and shabby, in 1987 when called into works where the expectation was that it would be repainted into blue. However, it reappeared in green with full yellow ends, the story being that this was on the express wish of the Chief Mechanical Engineer of the LM Region. Whatever the intent, this smart new green livery turned this locomotive into a celebrity and it was much in demand for enthusiast specials and attracted a lot of attention when seen in regular traffic.

Air horn vents (polished brass)

The two air horns in the nose were hidden behind two circular grilles and many locomotives ran with these unpainted and in some cases these were even polished.

Yellow warning panel, small

This was applied from early 1962. Some locomotives appear to have been delivered with the small panel in place; for example No D396 was observed in traffic with such a feature in July 1962 when brand new. The last locomotive built, a centre headcode example (No D399) was delivered in September 1962 with this style of warning panel, but with rounded top corners. It is not known to the author how many other locomotives were delivered new with small yellow end warning panels, although it is believed that the last 15 locomotives (D385 to D399) were delivered with these.

Some of the centre headcode examples had the panel with square corners (such as No D371) rather than rounded corners. There was some variation when the small yellow warning panel was applied to the disc headcode versions, with No D279 having the top of the panel level with the top of the marker lights while No D276 had the top halfway up the middle marker lights. The most common style was where the panel was level with the top of the marker lights. The locomotives modified by Haymarket with centre headcode panels (Nos D260 to D266) had a yellow warning panel which did not cover the complete nose end, but this was larger than the standard small panel which went around the centre headcode, but which was not a complete yellow end.

No D386 stands alongside a Class 47, No D1766, at York in 1965 showing rounded top corners to the yellow warning panel and two overhead warning flashes on the nose front. The bogie lubrication system is still in place and a shed plate is fitted under the number. The Class 47s replaced the Class 40s on Class 1 trains on the East Coast main line, although here the EE Type 4 has a Class 1 train indicated on the headcode box.
G. W. Sharpe

No D393 at Bradford showing a green liveried locomotive with full yellow nose, but a data panel has yet to be applied.
G. W. Sharpe

Yellow warning panel, large

From 1967 onwards, all locomotives had the whole nose front and a few inches on the nose top and sides painted yellow. In addition to blue-liveried locomotives, this also applied to those in green with some examples receiving the full yellow ends while still carrying the 'D' prefix to their number. Examples of green locomotives with full yellow ends included Nos D209, D215, 216 (1971), 218, 235, D241 (1971), D269, D295, 328, 333, 335, 343, D347, D348, D393, D396 (1967), 40010 (1974), 40022, 40052 and 40096,

Green-liveried No D287 has full yellow ends and a data panel below the number. The body side has evidence of patch repainting.
Author's collection

Locomotive numbers

When built, there were four sets of numbers carried – one on each cab side below the windows. These were in pale cream in the format Dxxx.

When steam was eliminated from the network in August 1968 the 'D' prefix of the number was painted out, eg D242 became plain 242. The decision was made in 1973 to renumber all diesel and electric locomotives with the class prefix under the TOPS classification (Total Operations Processing System), the English Electric Type 4s becoming Class 40.

Renumbering followed the format of dropping the leading '2' or '3' and putting the class number in front, so D201 became 40001. As the TOPS computer could not recognise 40000 (for D200), and as No D322 had already been withdrawn, No D200 was given the otherwise missing number 40122. The class was therefore renumbered as follows:

D201 to D321 = 40001 to 40121
D200   = 40122
D323 to D399 = 40123 to 40199

At this point, many of the class were still running in green, so subsequently a number of green-painted locomotives received the new 40xxx numbers including 40010, 40052, 40096, 40106, 40135, 40136, 40169, 40171, 40181 and 40189. The positioning of the new number varied. For example, Nos 40096 and 40181 had the number under the cab window, and 40190 (under the cab window, one end only), while 40039, 40052 and 40053 had their numbers on the other side of the cab door from the nose. Generally, the 40xxx was applied only once per side, adjacent to the driver's door.

When No 40106 was repainted in green, the numbers were applied to all four cab sides of the locomotive. The same was done when No 40122 (ex-D200) was returned to traffic after it had been repainted green, but in this case one end carried D200 and the other 40122.

Data panel

With the renumbering into Class 40, a data panel was fixed on the body side indicating which class the locomotive was, its maximum speed, brake force (in tons), route availability (RA) and weight (in tons). The data panel was a self-adhesive plastic sheet (not a stencil) and was applied to locomotives still in green livery, even if the 40xxx series number had not yet been applied. Again, the positioning varied, sometimes being below the cab window (Nos 40052, 216 (1971), D295 (1971), 40152 and 40181 (1974)), and on others it was on the other side of the cab doors, which was the more usual position. The background to the data panel was blue.

No 325 in green livery with full yellow ends and data panel under the number is depicted at Crewe Works in October 1969. *G. W. Sharpe*

No 335 in April 1974, still in green livery but with full yellow ends and a data panel below the number. Overhead warning flashes are fitted above the headcode boxes. The nose doors retains all the hinges and fittings. *G. W. Sharpe*

Traction motor indicator

When the traction motors were changed for a different type the modification was indicated to shed staff for a period by means of a pale blue bar painted under the number. This applied to both green- and blue-liveried locomotives. When this upgrade was completed and all members of the class were fitted with the revised motors the blue bar was no longer required and disappeared with subsequent repaints.

No D380 in green with small yellow warning panel (with rounded corners) and data panel under the number. The blue line below the number indicates the type of traction motor fitted. The bogie lubrication system is still installed under the cab door on the bogie side and two overhead warning flashes are fitted to the nose front. *Author's collection*

Allocation indicator

When the steam-style cast-iron shed code plates were abandoned, the region to which the locomotive was allocated was occasionally painted under the number, such as 'W' for Western Division of the LM Region, but sometimes this appeared as 'LM'.

Pipework colour code

The pipework in the locomotive was colour coded and some of the pipes were visible through the side windows. The codes were as follows:

Fire equipment – *Post Office red*

Lubricating oil – *salmon pink*
Fuel oil – *brown*
Cooling water – *Oxford blue*
Steam-heat boiler feed water – *green*
Compressed air and vacuum – *white*
Electrical conduits – *orange*
Waste oil and drainage – *black*

The colour-coded pipes and conduit were visible through the bodyside window. *Author*

Buffer beam pipework colour codes

Pipes on the buffer beam were also colour coded, as follows:

Vacuum train pipe – *red*
Steam-heat pipe – *silver*
Main reservoir air pipe – *white* (two pipes)

Regulating air pipe – *white* (two pipes)
Multiple working jumper and sockets – *orange* (both sides of coupling)

When converted to auto air-brake pipes:

Auto air-brake pipe – *red*
Main reservoir pipe – *yellow*

BR blue

The BR blue livery varied, mainly in the position and format of the locomotive numbers. The common factor was an all-over blue livery (including the roof) with full yellow ends and the new BR double arrow symbol at each end on the cab sides. The first application of this new British Rail scheme was in 1967 when locomotives still carried Dxxx series numbers.

When in blue livery, some locomotives had the buffer beam painted black, such as No 200.

No D248 at rest showing the first version of the blue livery, with the lettering style of the numbers replicating that of the numbers carried when in Brunswick green livery. Later during the blue era, the style of lettering used for the numbers was changed. The bar below the number, which was usually pale blue, denotes a change of traction motor type and was applied to aid maintenance staff. Double arrows are displayed at both ends.

Nos 97408 (ex 40118) and 97405 (ex 40060) pass Gresty on 3 June 1985 en route to Basford after refuelling at the depot. The axle boxes are painted yellow but no red band. *B. G. Hughes*

Running number positions

In the transition period between the original green livery and the final blue livery there were a number of transitional arrangements. The types of numbering styles were as below.

Dxxx numbers moved from the nose side of the cab door to the other side of the cab doors, lettering now white rather than cream. Examples included Nos D206 and D364.

a. From sometime in 1968, and onwards, the 'D' prefix was removed, leaving just the number, examples including Nos 200, 214, 216, 220, 250, 254, 262, 283, 313 and 330. This was often done at a shed and the unwanted letter was crudely painted over.

b. The original number changed from the three-digit figure to 40xxx from October 1973, and onwards, which took around 12 months to complete for the whole class. With this variant there was only one, small arrow symbol per side. When the 40xxx number was applied it appeared only once on each side, located adjacent to the driver's door.

c. During the 1980s, a number of locomotives had their original number added to the end opposite to the 40xxx number, so in 1982, No 40028 was observed with that number at one end and 228 at the other, located on the body side of the cab door.

d. In 1985, four withdrawn locomotives were reinstated to traffic specifically to work track renewal trains for the Crewe remodelling scheme and were given new,

No D261 displays the first rendering of the BR blue livery with double arrows at both ends, the 'D' number on the other side of the door to previously, and full yellow ends. The lettering style for the numbers is slightly different from that used on the green livery. This example has all the features of the Haymarket-allocated locomotives, the multiple working connections removed (and no blue stars on the nose), and the addition of the centre headcode box with square corners. At this date (c1967) there are no overhead warning flashes and it retains its bogie lubrication system.
Author's collection

No 291 demonstrates the early version of the blue livery with the BR double arrows at both ends and the 'D' prefixes deleted. The familiar BR logo was subsequently reduced to one per side. The water tanks clearly show the ribbing applied for strengthening, after they were built.
Locophoto Co

departmental numbers: 97405 (ex-40060), 97406 (40135), 97407 (40012) and 97408 (40118). By this time, No 97407 had three different running numbers displayed: 40012 in the normal position, 97407 further along the body side and 212 at the other end, along with its name *Aureol*, painted on a red background with white edging.

No 40079 is seen at Manchester Victoria in December 1984 on a parcels train and is numbered 279 at one end and 40079 at the other. Unusually, the data panel is under the cab window. It has a red buffer beam and the radiator frost grille has been removed. *G. W. Sharpe*

No 40028 at York station with an express with its original number (228) at the far end and the grille cover over the radiator removed.
G. W. Sharpe

No 97405 (ex-D260/40060) having been reinstated for civil engineering work. It carries 97405 on one end and 260 on the other. The multiple working connections have been removed and it displays a red buffer beam. *G. W. Sharpe*

Some locomotives had the numbers placed further along the body side (ie closer to the centre of the locomotive). Examples included Nos 40025 (1981), 40064, 40095 (1979). No 40010 was observed with the number on the nose, under the builder's plate (May 1974).

Late in their life, a number of locomotives had their numbers painted on the nose front, usually in the top third. As these were done by depots the location, spacing and style of lettering varied. Examples included Nos 40002, 40003, 40018, 40022, 40058 and 40069.

No 40108 is seen in October 1980 at Swindon showing the number and data panel further along the body side than was usual. *G. W. Sharpe collection*

Double arrow symbols

Positioning of the double arrow logo varied, and once the locomotives had received the 40xxx numbers the usual style was to have only one per side, although several locomotives received an arrow at each end, but still with only one locomotive number per side. Those identified were Nos 40040, 40041, 40051, 40052, 40089, 40097, 40112, 40125, 40152, 40156 and 40179.

A few locomotives were observed without any arrows at all, an example being No 40157.

No 40023 *Lancastria* is seen at Sheffield Midland on 28 July 1979. The name has been painted on the bodyside and there are double arrows at each end. The headcode discs indicate that it has come off or is about to work an express passenger train. The front grille has been removed from the radiator intake.
Author

Data panels

The data panel was usually positioned under the number which was on the body side to the right of the driver's door. As with the green-liveried examples, however, there were some variations. For example, Nos 40039 (1976), D360 (in blue), 40079 and 40152 had the data panel below the driver's window while the number was on the body side.

Several locomotives were observed without any data panel at all, including Nos 40015, 40028, 40075 and 40130.

As mentioned earlier, a small 'NB' was sometimes painted below the data panel indicating there was 'No Boiler'. Some locomotives had the NB painted to the right of the driver's door in the position previously occupied by the shed plate, as was certainly done for those allocated to Healey Mills (Wakefield), while others had it below the running number.

On the data panel:

Class		
Weight tonnes		13?
Brake force tonnes		5?
ETH index		
RA		6
Max speed mph		9?

Fire extinguisher operating handle

In blue livery, a number of locomotives were observed with the brass surround of the fire extinguisher operating handle painted in red, but when in green this had been very often unpainted. This was in fact the manual pull to operate the fire extinguisher system.

To operate the pull-handle involved breaking a glass cover. The CO_2 gas bottles used in the system needed to be locked out of use with pins to prevent accidental discharge when maintenance staff were inside the locomotive. If they went off accidentally the maintenance staff would have to get out pretty quickly, or be carried out!

The data panel applied to this and other classes was a self-adhesive label and was usually located under the number, but not in all cases. A blue sticker was used even on green-liveried locomotives. *Author*

Overhead warning flashes

These were introduced following trials at Colchester in March 1960 and they were fitted to both steam and diesel locomotives that would work under overhead wires. The usual placement was as follows:

Two on each nose end just below and to one side of the nose grilles.

One adjacent to the access door in the centre of the body, both sides.

However, when overhead warning flashes were first fitted, many locomotives had only

No D246 at Cleethorpes in July 1967 in green livery with small yellow warning panel and two overhead warning flashes on the nose front. The locomotive still has its bogie lubrication system fitted and has acquired vertical handrails on the nose corners. Even at this early date, the Stone steam-heat boiler exhaust port (immediately behind the cab) has been plated over. *G. W. Sharpe*

No D215 *Aquitania* on 28 July 1968 in green livery, but now with full yellow ends and black-painted grille covers to the two air horns. Two overhead warning flashes have been fitted to the nose front. The locomotive retained its nameplates after being repainted blue and still had them in 1973. *G. W. Sharpe*

one on each nose end, usually on the driver's side. Examples included Nos D217 (1961), D224 (1964), D231 (1961), D268, D307 (1963), D313 (1961), D314 (1961), D309 (1964), D316 and D354 (1962). By 1966, these had changed to two on the nose front. There were minor variations in the placement of these warning flashes on the body side adjacent to the centre access door with both sides being used. In a few cases one was placed either side of the door at the same time such as on Nos D216, D225 (both 1968), 40029 (1979) and 40068 (1977). One of the preserved examples shows signs that at different times the placement had switched sides. Late in their lives, additional warning flashes were also placed adjacent to the cab doors, on the right. Examples included Nos 40094, 40099 and 40144.

The Scottish Region was very slow in fitting warning flashes and some locomotives had still not been fitted by 1965, when the locomotives were in green livery.

Black edge to headcode disc

A number of locomotives were observed with the headcode disc edged in black.

Examples included No D253, when it was based at Gateshead. This practice continued throughout the life of the class and there were many other examples seen with this feature.

No 40012 showing black-edged headcode discs and how some depots applied the running number to the nose end. *Author*

40 012

Blue-liveried
No D298 on
10 April 1974 with
its headcode discs
edged in black.
The nose doors
have been welded
up and the hinges
and clips removed.
G. W. Sharpe

Shed allocation

When locomotives were in blue livery, some depots painted the shed name under the data panel.

No 40050, shown at York in July 1983, does not display a data panel but there is a shed allocation panel under the number. The running number is poorly applied in white lettering across the nose and additional overhead warning flashes are fitted adjacent to the nose. There are no double arrow symbols on the bodyside.
G. W. Sharpe collection

No D340 at Crewe on 28 October 1963 with its Crewe North (5A) shed plate fitted below the number. This locomotive has had the small yellow warning panel applied with two overhead warning flashes to the nose front. *[Author's collection*

Headcode display

In 1976, the display of headcode numbers on the locomotive to identify the train being worked was abandoned and the headcode blinds were removed and replaced by black and white 'domino' panels.

When train headcodes had been introduced it was not unusual for a disc-headcode locomotive to have the train reporting number displayed on the centre cab window.

Nameplates

The following locomotives were named shortly after entering service, with the plates applied between May 1960 and March 1963. The nameplates were cast aluminium for the first ones named but some plates were made of resin and painted to represent aluminium. (*Laconia*, named in 1962, is one such example, although the *Laconia* plate at York is cast aluminium yet the plate owned by Pete Waterman is cast in resin. Perhaps replacement plates were made.) They carried a representation of the flag of the ship above its name with the respective shipping line in smaller lettering underneath. (They were reminiscent of the Southern Railway's 'Merchant Navy' nameplates, but were

smaller.) The background of the plates was normally red, with the raised lettering polished aluminium.

It is not clear why these 25 locomotives were the only ones in the class named, but all referred to ocean liners with associations with the port of Liverpool. The bulk of these had the nameplates applied during workshop visits to Crewe and Derby, but a few had official naming ceremonies. These included No D210 *Empress of Britain*, named on 12 May 1960 at a ceremony at Euston station by N. R. Crump, President of the Canadian Pacific Steamship Co, No D211 *Mauretania*, unveiled at Liverpool Riverside station on 20 September 1960 by Sir John Brocklebank, Chairman of Cunard Lines, and No D212 *Aureol*, named on the same

An example of one of the nameplates applied to a small number of the class, in this case No 40012 (D212) *Aureol*. The plates were still carried by this locomotive following repainting into blue in 1971 when the number was amended to 212, without the 'D' prefix. The early plates were cast in aluminium, but later ones were made of resin and painted to look like polished aluminium. *Author*

No D210 when brand-new and named *Empress of Britain*, receiving its name at an official ceremony on 13 May 1960.

occasion, by Mr M. Glaister, a director of Elder Dempster Lines. Peter Hiley, a pattern-maker at Derby, made the patterns for *Mauretania* and *Aureol* many months before naming, and the patterns for *Empress of Canada* were made by his colleague Anthony Millington more than a year before the plates were fitted. The other engines received their names between March 1961 and March 1963, not exactly a rapid process. Whilst the style of plate was good, they were, in the author's opinion, undersized and a little lost against the vast bulk of the locomotive's body sides.

No D226 was intended to be named *Media* (Cunard Lines) and one of the plates is now owned by Pete Waterman, but there is no evidence these were carried by the locomotive in service. Why this was so is not now known although the story related to Pete Waterman was that the plates were fitted in the works but someone then realised the name related to a ship that had been sunk. It was believed that permission would have been needed from the next of kin of those on board, so the plates were removed before the locomotive was returned to traffic.

The nameplate of No D222 and cast in resin. It is not known if these were original plates or replacements. *Author*

D210 *Empress of Britain* (Canadian Pacific Steamships). Named on 12 May 1960.

D211 *Mauretania* (Cunard Lines). Named on 20 September 1960. Nameplates still carried when locomotive painted blue (1973).

D212 *Aureol* (Elder Dempster Lines). Named 20 September 1960. Nameplates still carried when locomotive painted blue (1970).

D213 *Andania* (Cunard Lines). Named at Crewe Works June 1962.

D214 *Antonia* (Cunard Lines). Named at Derby Works May 1961.

D215 *Aquitania* (Cunard Lines). Named at Crewe Works May 1962. Nameplates still carried when locomotive painted blue (1973).

D216 *Campania* (Cunard Lines). Named at Crewe Works May 1962. Nameplates still carried when locomotive painted blue (1974).

D217 *Carinthia* (Cunard Lines). Named at Crewe Works May 1962.

D218 *Carmania* (Cunard Lines). Named at Derby Works July 1961.

D219 *Caronia* (Cunard Lines). Named at Crewe Works June 1962.

D220 *Franconia* (Cunard Lines). Named at Crewe Works February 1963.

D221 *Ivernia* (Cunard Lines). Named at Derby Works March 1961.

D222 *Laconia* (Cunard Lines). Named at Crewe Works October 1962. One of the plates from this locomotive is on display at the National Railway Museum, York. The plate was still fitted in 1974 when locomotive painted blue and renumbered 40022.

D223 *Lancastria* (Cunard Lines). Named at Derby Works May 1961.

D224 *Lucania* (Cunard Lines). Named at Crewe Works August 1962.

D225 *Lusitania* (Cunard Lines). Named at Crewe Works March 1962.

D227 *Parthia* (Cunard Lines). Named at Crewe Works June 1962. Nameplates still carried when locomotive painted blue and renumbered 40027 (1974).

D228 *Samaria* (Cunard Lines). Named at Crewe Works September 1962.

D229 *Saxonia* (Cunard Lines). Named at Crewe Works March 1963.

D230 *Scythia* (Cunard Line). Named at Derby Works April 1961. Plate still carried when painted blue in 1972.

D231 *Sylvania* (Cunard Lines). Named at Crewe Works May 1962.

D232 *Empress of Canada* (Canadian Pacific Steamships). Named at Derby Works March 1961. Nameplates still carried when locomotive painted blue (1974).

D233 *Empress of England* (Canadian Pacific Steamships). Named at Derby Works September 1961. Nameplates still carried when locomotive painted blue (1973).

D234 *Accra* (Elder Dempster Lines). Named at Crewe Works May 1962. Nameplates still carried when locomotive painted blue (1972).

D235 *Apapa* (Elder Dempster Lines). Named at Crewe Works May 1962. It was still in green with full yellow ends and nameplate in 1974.

Name changes and replacement names

The original plates were removed in the 1970s, usually when the locomotives were still in green livery, but at least nine received blue livery and retained their original nameplates. At least two of these also received a 40xxx number while still carrying their nameplates. The latest recorded date I have for a nameplate still being carried is June 1974 on No 40016 *Campania*.

The following are the known examples in blue livery with nameplates and dates recorded where known (but not necessarily the final date): Nos 212 *Aureol* (6/1971), 215 *Aquitania* (8/1973), 216 *Campania* (6/1974), 219 *Caronia*, 40027 *Parthia* (3/1974), 40032 *Empress of Canada* (5/1974), 233 *Empress of England*, and 234 *Accra* (5/1972). After the plates were removed, many locomotives had the names stencilled on (sometimes with a red background) where the cast plates had been

located. This stencilled name was usually in a different form as it was in a rectangle. When No 40035 had its original name *Apapa* reapplied in paint it was stencilled above its running number.

In addition to the official names, a number of unofficial names appeared stencilled on the body sides during the 1970s. Those noted included:

40104 *Warrior*
40129 *Dracula*
40131 *Spartan*
40132 *Hurricane*
40134 *Andromeda*
40137 *Trojan*
40145 *Panther*
40164 *Lismore*

No 97405 (ex-40060) had a painted name in the style of one of the cast plates, which was *Ancient Mariner* with 'Coleridge Lines' underneath to denote the 'shipping company'. Obviously, someone at Crewe

An example of a painted name, replacing the original cast plates as indicated by the bolt holes. *Author*

No D218 is seen in green livery with full yellow ends at Warrington in June 1970. Note the data panel under the number, the two overhead warning flashes on either side of the access doors in the middle of the locomotive and the blue bar under the number. The name (*Carmania*) is still on the bodyside. *G. W. Sharpe*

Diesel Depot had a literary bent as Samuel Taylor Coleridge wrote the poem 'The Rime of the Ancient Mariner'.

In August 1984, following preservation,

No 40106 (D306) was named *Atlantic Conveyor* to commemorate the ship sunk in the Falklands War.

Builder's plates

These were located just under each of the cab windows (making four in total on each locomotive) and were generally retained until withdrawal, although the very last examples in traffic tended to have had these removed. They were cast brass which was then chrome plated and had a black-painted background. Many of the preserved examples now have the brass showing through the chrome.

One of the four builder's plates fitted, one under each cab window, this one referring to No D278. These were chrome-plated cast brass. *Author*

Shed code plates

When first put into service many of the class were allocated to depots which still had steam locomotives and the new diesels were fitted with the traditional oval pattern cast shed code plates as their steam brethren. These were normally attached at one end (either No 1 or No 2 ends) and usually under the locomotive's number. Depots known to have fitted these plates included Crewe North (5A), Liverpool Edge Hill (8A), Camden (1B), Carlisle Kingmoor (12A), Gateshead (52A) and York (50A). Most of these plates had a black background but some were observed with a red background. When these plates were removed many locomotives continued to carry the two bolts that had held the plate to the locomotive's body side. In some cases, the depot painted the shed name below the data panel, when painted blue.

Routes

When introduced, the class was seen on most parts of the East and West Coast main lines working passenger trains as far north as Aberdeen and Inverness. For a number of years they also monopolised the traffic on the North Wales coast and became popular on holiday excursion trains between Leeds and Scarborough and to Skegness. As they were cascaded down to parcels and freight work they could be seen over most of the LM and former North Eastern regions.

Following the introduction of the 'Deltics' and Class 47s on the Eastern Region main line the Class 40s were displaced from top-flight passenger work from King's Cross. An analysis of the principal express trains leaving the station in 1964 over a 24-hour period showed only two workings out of 42 using Class 40s as motive power. By 1966 an instruction was issued banning them from being used on any principal workings out of King's Cross due to the weight of the trains — usually between 11 and 14 coaches. The Eastern Region Class 40s were then used on many of the night goods service and some semi-fast passenger trains. The initial allocations of the lighter and more powerful Class 47s were to the Eastern and Western regions leaving the LMR with its Class 40s.

However, until the electrification to Euston was complete the LMR had to rely on the class as its principal motive power, and with the completion of the West Coast electrification the EE Type 4s gravitated to

Below and right:
Two headboards as carried by Class 40s when they headed the crack expresses, and now on display in a private collection. The pattern for the 'Caledonian' was made at Derby works by Peter Hiley. *Author*

the North Wales main line and to freight duties.

As the class cascaded to freight and excursion duties they appeared in parts of the country where they had not been seen before, such as Gloucester, Oxford, Worcester, Welshpool and Severn Tunnel Junction. As late as 1981, driver training was conducted on the type for Severn Tunnel Junction crews as the class was being used on Mossend (Glasgow) and Crewe to South Wales freight services via Hereford.

No D229 heads the 8.23 Workington to Euston service, passing the site of Brinklow station on the Trent Valley line on 6 August 1961.
M. Mensing

No D231 is seen on the 2.5 Euston–Liverpool Lime Street leaving Stafford station, then under going reconstruction, on 4 March 1961.
M. Mensing

No D330 approaches Brinklow on the up Sunday 'Royal Scot' on 6 August 1961.
M. Mensing

Allocations

The first batch of engines, Nos D200 to D209, was allocated to the Eastern Region with Nos D200 and D202 to D205 allocated to Stratford for the Liverpool Street–Norwich services, with No D201 and D206 to D209 going to Hornsey for use on King's Cross trains.

The next batch, Nos D210 to D236, was allocated to the London Midland Region, being split between all the principal West Coast sheds including Crewe North, Camden, Liverpool (Edge Hill) and Manchester (Longsight).

Nos D237 to D254 and D256 to D259 were allocated to the North Eastern Region, at York and Gateshead.

Nos D260 to D266 and D357 to D368 were allocated to the Scottish Region at Edinburgh (Haymarket).

Nos D267 to D269, D287 to D344 and D369 to D384 went to various London Midland sheds including Crewe North and Liverpool (Edge Hill).

Nos D270 to D286, D349 to D356 and D385 to D399 were allocated to York and Gateshead while Nos D345 to D348 went to Leeds (Neville Hill), all on the North Eastern Region.

Once they began to be more frequently used on freight trains, the Class 40s were allocated to other depots, such as Healey Mills (Wakefield), Thornaby (Middlesbrough), Springs Branch (Wigan) and Tinsley (Sheffield). Leeds (Holbeck) had an allocation for working trains, both passenger and freight, over the Settle and Carlisle line.

During the initial deliveries a number of locomotives were temporarily allocated to sheds purely for crew-training purposes, such as in July 1960 when No D233 (1B, Camden) was allocated to Aston (Birmingham) and No D233 again to Holyhead in November 1960.

No 40191 was allocated to Hereford on the Western Region from June to November 1967, probably for crew training purposes when the class started working freights to South Wales.

Allocations by year

Nov 1961	Oct 1965	Dec 1968	Mar 1974	Nov 1979
10 Stratford	10 Stratford (Longsight)	51 Manchester Div	53 Longsight (Manchester)	48 Longsight (Manchester)
23 Camden	30 Camden (Wakefield)	47 Liverpool Div	33 Healey Mills (Wakefield)	22 Healey Mills (Wakefield)
14 Longsight (Manchester)	12 Willesden (Kingmoor)	12 Preston Div	26 Carlisle (Kingmoor)	13 Carlisle (Kingmoor)
16 Edge Hill (Liverpool)	17 Crewe North	20 Stoke Div	40 Springs Branch (Wigan)	36 Springs Branch (Wigan)
8 Carlisle (Upperby)	11 Rugby	12 Gateshead	8 Gateshead	20 Thornaby
1 Newton Heath (Manchester)	17 Bletchley	23 Healey Mills (Wakefield)	21 York	10 York
27 Crewe North	9 Carlisle (Upperby)	15 York	18 Haymarket (Edinburgh)	7 Gateshead
26 Gateshead	9 Longsight (Manchester)	18 Haymarket (Edinburgh)		26 Haymarket (Edinburgh)
21 York	7 Thornaby	1 Glasgow (Eastfield)		
4 Leeds (Neville Hill)	27 Gateshead			
14 Haymarket (Edinburgh)	32 York			
	19 Haymarket (Edinburgh)			

Royal Train working

The LM Region regularly used the class to haul the Royal Train, with Nos D216 and D225 (both in blue livery) being used for visits to the North West in 1968. Nos D216 and D233 (both in blue livery) were used for the Prince of Wales's investiture train to Caernarfon in 1969. Crewe Diesel Depot was usually given the responsibility for preparing the motive power for such workings and an excellent job they did, with the locomotives gleaming. However, the use of the class on these duties ceased in 1971, when the train was upgraded and thereafter required electric train heating.

Foreign travels

The class was extremely well travelled with most parts of the BR network seeing the class at some point. The only areas not to see them on a regular basis were the South West (Devon and Cornwall) and the Southern Region, although the odd special did penetrate both areas. In 1958, No D201 ran from Doncaster to Farnborough on the

Southern Region with a special train, and in 1967, No D326 worked through to Southampton from Birkenhead. The class was popular for enthusiast specials and examples of the class were seen at Exeter in 1979 (Nos 40081 and 40084), Newton Abbot in 1977 (Nos 40081) and Portsmouth in 1978 (No 40173).

An unidentified member of the class is seen near Wennington on the Settle to Carlisle line working a special train in the 1980s. (The author took this photograph while waiting for a steam special!) *Author*

Repair locations and servicing

When the locomotives were first introduced they were allocated to depots which still had substantial steam allocations, including Stratford, Camden and Edge Hill which were not really suited to the servicing and inspection of diesel locomotives. On the LM Region the recently built Crewe Diesel Depot, opened in 1957, was given the task of carrying out examinations and repairs for all EE Class 40s on the region, covering Camden, Carlisle, Manchester (Longsight) and Liverpool (Edge Hill) depots. This enabled servicing and repairs to be carried out in a much cleaner environment and with specially trained fitting staff, which was particularly important during the early days in traffic when there were a number of teething troubles to be rectified.

The main works responsible for the repair of the Class 40s were initially Crewe and Doncaster. Other workshops also carried out repairs, including Stratford and Derby (from 1961), where several locomotives received their names during overhaul in the early 1960s.

Withdrawals

The first member of the class to be withdrawn was No D322 in December 1967 following a major accident at Warrington in May 1966. The next locomotives to be withdrawn were Nos 40189 and 40190 (Springs Branch) in January 1976, while later that month Nos 40005, 40039 (still in green livery), 40102 (all Healey Mills) and 40043 Manchester (Longsight) were also taken out of service. During the rest of 1976 individual locomotives were withdrawn from Manchester (Longsight), Gateshead and Edinburgh (Haymarket). In 1977 a further four locomotives from York and Edinburgh (Haymarket) were retired, followed by another in 1978. Things then settled down until 1980 when withdrawals started again and proceeded at a pace, so that by the end of 1982 half the class had been withdrawn. The remaining examples tended to be dual vacuum and air braked, but by the beginning of 1985 there were only 17 members of the class in traffic, but this was not to be for long and all were withdrawn by that March except No D200/40122, which was not finally withdrawn until 1988.

Disposal

Following withdrawal, some bogies from Class 40s were reused and modified for snowplough duties. Just after the remainder of the class had been withdrawn, as previously stated, four were reinstated to traffic for the Crewe remodelling scheme in 1985, and once this had been completed they were used on civil engineering trains for a few months before being finally withdrawn in 1986 and 1987.

Locomotives were cut up at BR workshops and by private scrap contractors at the following locations: Crewe Works, Swindon Works, Doncaster Works, Derby Works, Vic Berry in Leicester and Thomas W. Ward at Inverkeithing. In one case, a locomotive was scrapped in the same yard as a ship after which one of its sister locomotives had been named.

Seven of these magnificent engines have been preserved as follows:

Locomotive Nos	Preserved by	Current location	Operational status	Notes
D200 (40122)	National Railway Museum	North Yorkshire Moors Railway	Operational	Restored in full BR green with small yellow warning panel. On loan to the NYMR 2005-08.
D212 *Aureol* (40012/97407)	Class 40 Appeal	Midland Railway Centre	Operational	In the process of being repainted into BR green, 2005/06. Nose ladders reinstated.
D213 *Andania* (40013)	Trevor Dean	Barrow Hill Roundhouse	Under restoration	Still in original (40013) faded blue livery.
D306 (40106)	Gerald Bowden	Nene Valley Railway	Operational	In BR green with full yellow ends. Named *Atlantic Conveyor*. Nose ladders reinstated.
D318 (40118/97408)	16SVT Society	Tyseley Railway Museum	Under restoration	
D335 (40135/97406)	Class 40 Preservation Soc	East Lancs Railway, Bury	Operational	In BR green. Split headcode box.
D345 (40145)	Class 40 Preservation Soc	East Lancs Railway, Bury	Operational (main line)	In BR blue. OTMR fitted and with standard square headlights. Centre head code box.

The reinstatement of a number of Class 40s for departmental use in May 1985 undoubtedly assisted in the preservation of three of these engines as they were not withdrawn until 1986, with the last one, No 97408, not being withdrawn until March 1987. These became celebrity locomotives and also ensured that a split headcode type was preserved so that all three variants of nose end have survived.

The big news in 2002 was the return to main line traffic of No D345/40145. It has been used on a number of special trains on the main line on a regular basis to many different destinations on the national network — and long may it continue to do so. In early 2006 it became the first diesel locomotive owned by a preservation society to be fitted with OTMR data recording equipment.

Privately owned No 40106, now based on the Nene Valley Railway, has had its nose ladder reinstated and had the name *Atlantic Conveyor* bestowed in 1984.
Garry Sparks

The Class 40 Preservation Society's main line No 40145 at Bristol Temple Meads on 4 June 2005 with the 'Whistling Slater', destined for Blaenau Ffestiniog.
Matthew Stoddon

The preservation of No D200

As the end of the EE Type 4s in BR service approached, questions were being asked if the class leader, No D200 (40122), would be preserved, but the National Railway Museum stated it had no intention of accepting such a locomotive for posterity on behalf of the nation. Following a main generator failure, No 40122 was withdrawn in August 1981 and was stored at Carlisle in readiness for towing to Crewe or Swindon for scrapping. Fortunately, the locomotive was held back by the LM chief mechanical engineer in the expectation that it would either be preserved or restored to traffic for enthusiast workings.

However, the locomotive had a large number of faults and therefore was not an attractive proposition for a preservation group and the National Railway Museum remained silent on whether it could offer the locomotive a home. The months and years rolled by and many alternative schemes were proposed, eventually resulting in BR agreeing to a depot overhaul using components from other Class 40s to keep the costs down, with the locomotive to be used for enthusiast specials as well as ordinary traffic.

By this time, No 40122 had a significant advantage over its green celebrity sister, No 40106, in that it was dual braked, so the latter was withdrawn with the remaining vacuum braked '40s' in March 1983 while in May 1983, the doyen of the class arrived at Toton depot for its long overdue overhaul. No 40072 was used to provide spares including the engine and generator set and

Now owned by the Class 40 Preservation Society, No 40145 is today the only member of the class certificated for main line running. It heads a Pathfinder Tours train, the 'Whistling Slater' from Bristol to Blaenau Ffestiniog on 4 June 2005 as it climbs the Lickey incline. This was its second return to the main line in preservation, following a major overhaul costing in excess of £50,000 and including a 10-year body lift. The work was carried out at Barrow Hill roundhouse.

Simon Stephens

No D200, as the
'grey ghost' hurtling
out of the mist at
Tamworth Low Level
with what turned
out to be the final
run before
withdrawal.
P. Tandy

one complete bogie unit. The overhaul was completed in July 1983 with the locomotive now fully repainted in its original green livery with full yellow ends and bearing the number D200 at one end and 40122 at the other. The depot went to great lengths to return the locomotive to its original condition, including restoring the outer frost grille and painting the buffer beam red.

On its return to traffic No D200/40122 worked normal freight diagrams as well as its enthusiast trains and it outlived its fellow class members by three years, finally being withdrawn in April 1988. It was then presented to the National Railway Museum who had finally agreed to give it a home. Maintained in operational condition, it visited several heritage railways and railway events and then went on loan to the North Yorkshire Moors Railway in 2005. This stay has been extended by a two-year agreement made early in 2006.

The preservation of this historic locomotive therefore came about only as a result of a number of people not giving up and keeping it in the spotlight by persuading BR to put it back into traffic and the NRM to finally accept it, and the dedication and enthusiasm of the Toton staff who overhauled her. Gentlemen, we thank you all.

Conclusion

The English Electric Type 4s were simple and solid locomotives, and after the steam-heat boilers were sorted out, quite reliable; after all, unreliable locomotives are not put on Royal Trains! The electrical system was very simple and straightforward, with relays and contactors that could be seen moving and therefore easier to fault find. Modern diesel locomotives are full of black boxes, printed circuit boards and software making fault diagnosis much more difficult. The engines were simple and rugged (if not particularly powerful) and importantly, unlike many of the Pilot Scheme locomotives, were reliable. Some of those early Pilot Scheme locomotives spent most of their lives on shed being repaired, the Clayton Type 1 and the Metrovic Co-Bo Type 2s being among the worst examples.

The Class 40s may now appear as overweight dinosaurs, but they were an important step in the development of diesel-electric traction on Britain's railway network and, once heard, the sound of that fabulous engine will never be forgotten.

The societies involved with the preservation of Class 40 locomotives deserve support and many of them have excellent websites:

http://tyseley.40118-web.co.uk for the 16SVT Society based at Tyseley, Birmingham.

www.cfps.co.uk for the Class 40 Preservation Society based at Bury (custodians of Nos D335 and 40145).

http://www.trainweb.org/cfa/ for the Class 40 Appeal based at the Midland Railway–Butterley (custodians of No D212 *Aureol*).

Overleaf: No D203 approaches Witham with the 1.45pm Norwich-Liverpool Street service on 7 November 1960.
M. Edwards

The first three Class 40s built: No D200 as restored to green livery, No 40001 (D201) and 40002 (D202) at Carlisle. No 40001, which had been withdrawn at the time of the photograph, has the headcode discs removed.
G. W. Sharpe

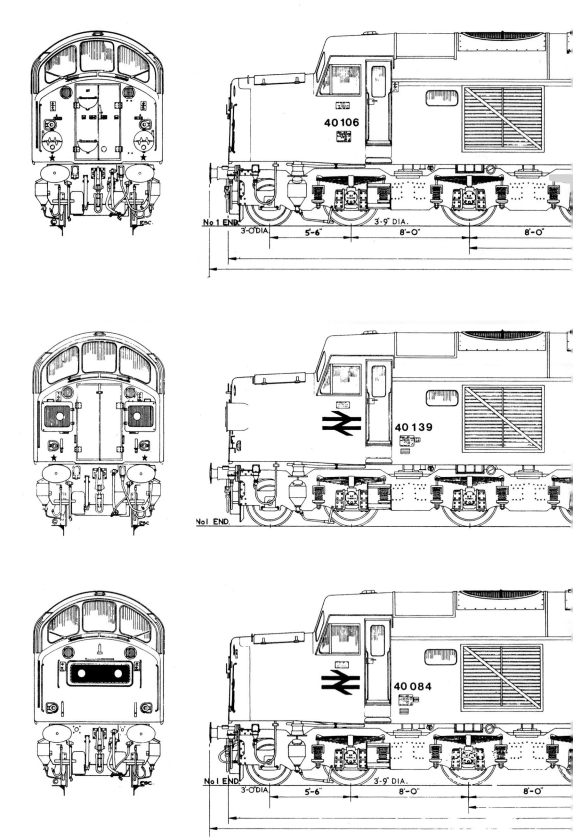

Drawings by the late Russell Carter

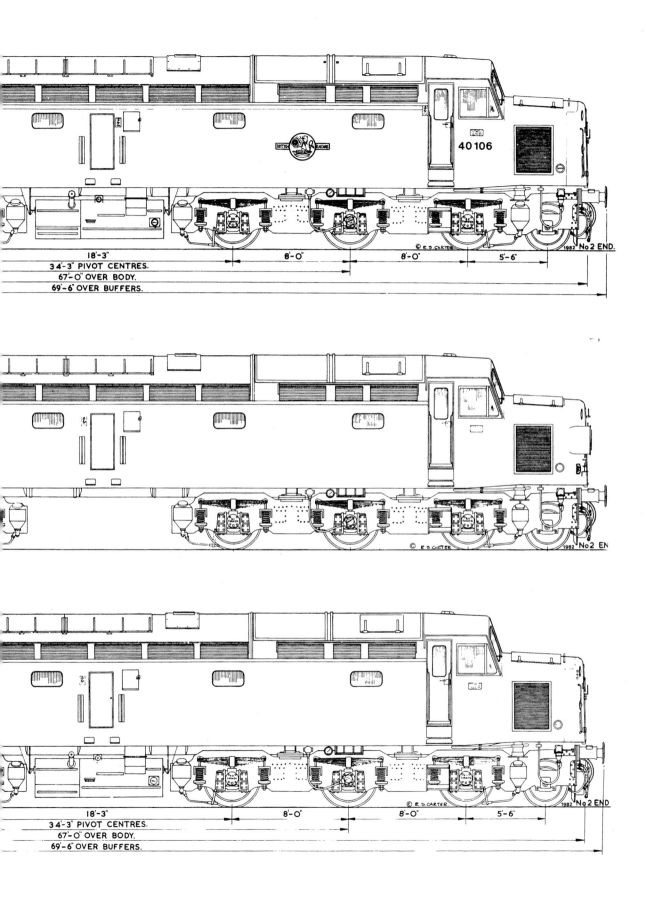

40 106

18'-3"
8'-0"
8'-0"
5'-6"
No 2 END.
© R. S. CARTER 1982

34'-3" PIVOT CENTRES.
67'-0" OVER BODY.
69'-6" OVER BUFFERS.

© R. S. CARTER 1982   No 2 EN

18'-3"
8'-0"
8'-0"
5'-6"
© R. S. CARTER 1982   No 2 END

34'-3" PIVOT CENTRES.
67'-0" OVER BODY.
69'-6" OVER BUFFERS.